SIMPLY STATED...

SOLE *TO* SOUL

Limited
Edition

BALETTE HINES

SIMPLY STATED...
SOLE *TO* SOUL

Limited
Edition

RP

REALIZATION
ᔥ PRESS ᘓ

Republished by Realization Press 2021

Cover design by Tonya Monique Swain Aniton
Interior design by Simply B! LLC

Published in the United States of America
ISBN: 978-1-944662-59-2
Biography & Autobiography / Women

Contents

Introduction

YOU KNOW THE sayings every woman has her moment and every dog has his day, but did you know every shoe serves its own particular purpose? I have always had a very fond love of shoes since before I can remember, and like most young girls, it started out with the wearing of your momma's old high heel shoes around the house to make you feel pretty while playing dress up, and then as you get in your teens you want to know what you would look like a little taller and sometimes a bit more sophisticated; but in the back of every girl's mind you want to really know, is there anything other than comfort that can be found in a pair of shoes?

Now when I say comfort, it can come across as many different things. You can find comfort in an old blanket, a place you're familiar with, or even a person for that matter, but I, however, find comfort in shoes. From the open toe heels, a four-inch stiletto, to the elegant pumps, evening shoes, and yes, of course, the boots—ankle boots, cuff length boots, calf-length boots, knee-high boots, thigh-high boots, and the infamous waist-high boots for those that want to take it that far. If you ever want to see how rough a road is in someone's life, take a walk in their shoes…NOT! I have my own shoes to fill and my own path to take, so find the shoe that fits you!

Now, ladies, I know you're wondering what the hell does buying a pair of shoes have to do with anything, and the honest answer is nothing; they cost a pretty penny if you get the right ones; you may sometimes end up with buyer's remorse, depending on your reasoning for the purchase, or you buy a pair that will leave a lasting imprint in your mind as well as your closet. I have never been into name brands or even the flashy shoes for that matter, just that one that stood out amongst the others. Some women have a weird sense, kind of like "shoetuition" when they see a shoe. Some, like myself, can visualize a complete outfit before it's purchased, the effects, rants, raves, and reviews before the shoe is even rang up and all this while styling that left or right leg in what about an eight inch mirror to check it out…HELLO! I used to use to believe dating was like looking for a good pair of shoes; you try on a few, purchase a few, and eventually you find that pair that suits you right and just can't be without somewhere in your wardrobe.

Standing only five foot two, I never viewed boots as a necessity in my wardrobe because I personally thought they made my legs look shorter, so my closet consisted of almost every type of shoe except boots other than the work-related combat boots. Sure I had seen plenty of girls wearing boots—in the winter time that is—but coming from down south, the weather isn't exactly screaming for boot season. As I learned in my journey called womanhood, regardless of the weather or the environment, sometimes a great pair of boots will get you through this thing called life.

Men and shoes, a heck of a comparison, but they seem to be my weakness and my strength. I am a woman of many hats and lives, and I enjoy them all. I am the lady of the night that loves to walk on the wild but exotic side, the heartbreaker, the adulterer, the romantic, and the lover, but most of all I am a woman. A woman with flaws and pain that life could not cover; but what love couldn't mask, sex made better. As I grew up, I grew out and learned to master this game called love, life, and the laughter. So walk into my closet and see the variety but try not to judge the outcome. Besides, they're only shoes, right?

Life can be compared to a closet, and for some, it is like a walk-in closet full of variety where you can walk in and transform yourself into anyone you want to be physically. Your closet allows you to speak without saying words, hear without listening, but most of all it shows you a trend when you refuse to see it on your own. As women, we sometimes get lost in our closets, and we call it our place of refuge or that place when you walk in you can sometimes see your past, present, and future. At what point in life do you realize it's time to come out of the closet and show the world that this is you and that you are here? It is at that precise moment when you realize you are now one with yourself, and you can now walk in your closet and see it for more than the four walls and immense gallery of shoes but for life.

As I walk through the front door, tired from yet another day, I lay my keys on the counter as I normally do, leave the shoes of the day against the wall, drop my bag in the chair at my work desk, make a stop in the bathroom to remove my jewelry, change into something comfortable, and I head to my closet. Along the way I grab my laptop, it is time to do inventory. I glance around and notice there are some items I can't quite get rid of just yet; some have memories in which closure is inevitable and a few others are stored occupying space. Ever wonder what your life would have been like if there was no change or think about the what-ifs, look back, and have regrets on things that went wrong and try to piece together what you could have done to make it better now that you know better? The should've, would've, could've is what my mom would always call it. In life, God puts you on a path, and he allows you to make mistakes in my thought process. He does this to show you he is in control and that nothing can be accomplished without him. What about when you lose faith and you start to pave your own road? I can remember thinking that if God didn't want this to happen, then he would stop it or at least step in and give me a sign. Maybe he did and I just overlooked it, or I just didn't know what sign I should have been looking for... but once again I am rambling on and on because I am a procrastinator of sorts. Looking around the closet, all I can think about is, *Man, this is going to be an all-nighter, but I got this far, so I might as well open the door and walk in.* I turn to glance in the full-length mirror that sits in the corner of my closet, say a short prayer, and I begin. First we have to separate the shoes, starting with the sneakers and tennis shoes.

Brandy. Fun, loveable, and naive, that quiet and shy girl everyone wanted to know about. Raised by a single mother and the youngest of four girls, she learned the knocks of life very early on. Her entire teenage life was spent in a strict lifestyle that was so organized that when the bells of freedom started to ring, she wanted to explore. Now we move on to an assortment of boots. Simone, a soldier in every aspect of the word, she led a life so disciplined that it was almost controlling. She was that chick that every guy wanted to know. Beautiful inside and out and what most would call sweet, but she had a fearless sense about her and a thirst to find love. Dominique was that one that go-to pump or that one shoe that gave you so much comfort. She was the one that everyone thought had it all, but she was broken, beat down from life's constant obstacles in love. She lost the urge to live, to love, and for laughter, but she had others depending on her, and the overwhelming pressures would soon bring her to a crossroad. And then our stiletto, Tatiana, she was the man-eater, independent, educated with a strong sense of self; she was the real deal, and she could walk into a room and make time stop but, yet, struggled to find her place in this world. Four women of distinct character and personality but they shared one common goal, love, success, and spiritual freedom, a need to reach elevated nuance; but they faced each other to get there, and sometimes the woman on the other side of the mirror was just a mere reflection of just how damaged they were from the sole to the soul.

Brandy

YOUNG AND NAIVE in every aspect of the words, facing the world and life was something I was not prepared for. I grew up in a very strict and disciplined household where Momma's word was law and daddy was a wallet and a joke, but to me he was my savior and best friend. I must say I was raised by my mother, a strong, independent black woman who would always remind me that, "You can't depend on nobody in this world other than your sisters and me. Friends come and go, but we are forever. As a matter of fact, you ain't even got no friends. They are associates." I am the youngest of four girls, had my first kiss at nine, thought it was gross, first crush at eleven, first so-called boyfriend at thirteen, first date was senior prom, but through it all I knew that I would never let a man deter me from a promise I made my mom: "I will not have sex till after I graduate high school," a promise I intended to keep well beyond because my only concern was basketball and books. While my friends were enjoying the spoils of senior life, I was comfortable sitting around at home, and I dreamt of what life would be like after high school. I was scared of leaving the nest, however, because then I would be alone, but I wanted to see the world. After graduation I wanted to go away, dreamed of Colorado and how different life would be up there, but mom thought it best for me to stay close to home.

The first two weeks of college was lonely and full of tears. I lost touch with old friends and gained new ones. Soon thoughts of wanting to go home would quickly settle down, and I adjusted to this new environment. By adjust I mean adapt. I found a way to fit in without getting caught up in the social scenes. I would go to class every day, study with friends or a tutor at night, and that was my life, and I was loving not being told when to come home or what to do...finally my life was undisciplined and unstructured, but I was still doing what I knew had to be done. College life opened my life to a lot of freedoms, like drinking, smoking, and guys. I fell for him hard. There was no denying it. The mention of his name, to see him walk across the quad, or bump into him in the dorms made my heart beat a thousand miles per hour. He was tall, athletic, and had a smile that would make you melt...this was my running shoe, Brooks. Little did I know running shoe would fit him well. I mean they're good to walk in, run in, and work out, but soon you have to change the inserts from odor or throw them out. Brooks made me feel things that I didn't know existed inside of me. We had conversations that would have me in my dorm room thinking on a grown woman status. I wanted him, but I wanted him to love me in the emotional way. Sex had never been a topic of conversation for me because it was something during this time I was just not into, and when it was brought up, I felt a sense of discomfort and would excuse myself...first sign of a virgin quickly became my first mistake as I would see it, and he would take advantage of that moment, that thought, that emotion, and bring me to a point so low that even being ashamed was one up on me.

Now, ladies, you know when you shop for tennis shoes, you want the best; regardless of the brand, you want comfort and fit and then the salesperson comes over and tries to sell you the more expensive brand, and you keep saying no but they keep insisting till you're at the register with the pair the salespersons wanted you to have, and you walk out knowing it was wrong but blame yourself because it was on clearance and can't be returned, and then you hear them talking about the sale as you walk out the door. Well, meet Mr. Brooks, my passion became my pain. What a naive young girl thought was love was lust, and something beautiful became something ugly. My grades dropped, I was advised to see a psychiatrist, and even she had me convinced that I was wrong along with advisors. I was now damaged and broken, but most of all, I was heartbroken. Not only could I not look at this man the same, but I lost the innocence of the girl in the mirror, and I laced up my tennis shoes and ran. Running, something I was so used to doing and seeing others do that it became second nature for me. I decided to go back home after only a short time in college. I became that scared girl, and all I wanted was to be home, but it was more than that. This college experience had begun to change me in ways that I did not see or know until it was too late.

As I lay in the bed one day, I remember the tears starting to fall, the flashbacks and memories started to appear, and then suddenly it was dark. I had entered into a phase in life that I was unsure of…I was ashamed of everything from the way I looked to the way I dressed; my mind was so shattered, and my heart was crushed, and I just needed to find something, anything, to relieve myself from this pain. I awakened in a sweat, opened my door to see my mom's door was closed, which meant she was probably gone. I walked to the bathroom and looked at this face in the mirror that now looked so unfamiliar. One moment I was looking at her, the next she had convinced me I was worthless, and I grabbed the razor from the cabinet, and I slowly began to make a small cut; but it wasn't until I sliced it enough that blood came that I felt some type of relief. I realized after several episodes of doing this that I had found the answer to my pain, what I had gone through, and the way I handled it and how I felt weak, worthless, and unfocused. Each time I would cut, the immediate sting was suddenly stopped but the blood continued to run, and I was the source to my own pain. Now, ladies imagine, most of us when we purchase a pair of running shoes, we are looking for several details when it comes to wear and tear, but what happens when those shoes are worn out? This is the stage I had entered. Each time I cut myself, I envisioned running and falling. I would get up with a few scratches and scrapes and clean up the blood and continue. The wound itself would clear up, but the thought was still there, and me knowing it happened didn't change: anything. This is where the normal young woman would realize she was still the same young woman entering college regardless of what happened and to just clean up the wound and move on to be stronger and learn from it…but not me—I went the opposite direction.

Misery loves company, and I had become her best friend. By this time I was only one hundred pounds, and the cutting thing had subsided because I finally realized that I was only hurting myself more, so I focused on something else: my image, and began taking diet pills in mass quantities on a daily basis. Friends would talk about how skinny and small I was, but because I worked out a lot, they never would have known what was going on behind closed doors. Hell, I didn't even know what was going on because I was so out of it half the time, and I was so far gone from that smart, innocent Brandy. Months went by with me doing the same routine—clubbing every night, sleeping all day—until one day I woke and decided I needed to take responsibility for my actions and try to find control and a safe place within myself; better yet, I was on a quest to find me again.

After a seven-month hiatus on the dark side, I decided that it was time to once again step into the light. I enrolled back in college—somewhere nobody knew me, the family name, or my past—somewhere I can start fresh and recreate myself and my image. It's funny how when you put a plan together, you have this false sense of control like you did something. I put myself in a new environment in which the players in the game were foreign to me, but I did not go unnoticed. Everything started on an upbeat, and this is what we call the Nike phase, as their slogan states, "Just do it." I did just that. I went to class, met friends, partied, had met someone, and for a while I had it all under control, but it's at that point when memories of the past started to overwhelm me. I'm not good enough for him, I'm damaged, if he only knew, I began to push him away, and at that point love was not what I was looking for anymore. I didn't want anyone to hold me or embrace me to say it will be okay. I wanted someone else to feel the pain I was feeling inside carrying these burdens. We parted but remained friends, and seeing him around other women made a very angry person in me develop; now those things I once watched people do, I was partaking in. I would say I smoked about a pack of cigarettes a day, probably was doing it wrong, but hell, it didn't matter, I was drinking on a daily basis and sometimes showing up for class with a hangover if I even showed up at all. Money was tight, so I did what I had to do at times to make ends meet. I was sleeping with two members of the basketball team at the same time, although I tried to keep it on the down, but people knew. I think I even slept with one of their family members knowingly. I would make out with random strangers, phone calls home became rare to none, trips across the border were a must, and I was having a great time and thought I had the perfect life, but something was missing and I had to find it—I needed to find it. I wanted to go to a place to find me, and the more I thought about it, my past was affecting me so much more than I knew because I was acting out a lifestyle that I thought I didn't know; but the deeper I got into it, I began to think maybe this is the real me, maybe this is what I needed to see or to experience in order to get myself together. I was now experiencing pain and pleasure, hurt and comfort and all of those things your parents shield you from...I was experiencing the curiosities and the road less travelled, and I had my backpack and walking shoes ready for the journey.

Somewhere along the journey I began to forget, not really forget, but I got to a point where I could focus on life and had pushed history so far behind that I could put up a well put together front of a happy and content woman. As the music played, I closed my eyes and moved my body to the beat. I saw the various strange faces in the audience, but I didn't pay them any mind. All I can remember is I wanted to dance. I watched as so-called friends would walk by sniffling and wiping their noses constantly. I watched them as they would turn to each other for emotional and physical support and companionship. I watched women that I thought were so beautiful become so ugly, and then I saw me…Enough is enough. This is not the me I came to find. I enjoyed fulfilling my physical needs whether it was with him or her, and I embraced lessons and actions, but it was time to grow up and prepare, because the future I saw years ago was now starting to reveal itself again. So I put on my Huaraches and ran forward to it.

Now once again, ladies, you have found a great pair of shoes, and then outsiders throw out a new brand and tell you these are better that you should try them; and most times we do because we are in that societal trending phase. So I found and purchased a great pair of Converse…you know, the one where they have the same look just with a variety of colors; and boy, was he a variety. Converse was tall, dark, and handsome, had an athletic build, and a quiet shyness that seemed all too familiar. The familiarity was me. It was like time had been frozen, and we were meant to meet at this precise moment in each other's lives. We were inseparable, and it was just what I needed to move on. I had gotten to a point where I didn't recognize the young lady looking back at me in the mirror. With Converse it was different. That's the variety. He brought out that young lady in me that was so far gone back to a place of innocence and comfort. In him, I once again felt the need to love and want to be loved. My weekends weren't complete without him, and my nights were long. We spent hours on the phone talking about everything. The sex was amazing because now there was an emotion, and I welcomed it and him.

I remember walking around the house all day in a T-shirt waiting for him to come home and sleeping in the guest rooms at his job while he was on duty and him coming to see me on every break or chance he could to get away. He made me feel alive, a high that I couldn't get in the club or with a blunt. Hell, he was my blunt. Now the problem with Converses was that if you got the all-white ones, they got dirty easily; and the other colors, they would just fade, and we were approaching that point. During one of my many visits, I started to notice he was acting a bit differently, more possessive and controlling as far as when I could come down and calling him before I could show up. So one morning as I was making the bed, I noticed a letter under his mattress. I know, I know. If you look for trouble, you are bound to find it, and what I found made my heart drop. Now this weekend was supposed to be special, but I had not gotten around to talking with him yet, but I now questioned it...I was pregnant. But from what I read in the letter, he already had a baby that was just born and apparently a whole other life that I knew nothing about. That night we argued, and I wanted to believe him—I had to believe him. I loved him. I loved him so much that I couldn't tell him I was carrying his child; we were already slowly drifting away.

I returned to school and a friend told me my options because she had been down that road and was a single mother, something I was not ready to be. I decided this would be my little secret, and no one would ever have to know. That following spring semester, I decided to leave school. My GPA was practically nonexistent because I was no longer attending classes. I always seemed to be drained and tired, so I went back home to stay with my mom until I could get back on track. Converse and I still were hanging in there, but there was a slight distance between us.

The summer following me leaving school, I told him I was going to Georgia to stay with my sister for a few weeks because my mom and I were not getting along, mostly because I had been out of the house for almost two years now; and to have to live by someone else's rules was absurd and not in my plan. It hadn't even been a week that I was gone before I received that dreaded phone call. On the other end was a voice I had never heard but a name that was so familiar, and I felt my heart and the phone drop as she told me, "I am the mother of his son and his fiancée. I am sorry for any pain this may have caused you, but you are still young and will get over it." All I could do was touch my stomach as I felt the pain in my heart. I gave this man all of me, and I was now pregnant with his child, the stress and pain was too much to bear mentally and physically...I miscarried, and then I laced up my Converses, cleaned them up as much as I could, and placed them in a box; and it was at that point I decided to never let a man get that close to me that I could end up hurt again.

I cried for a day or two, and when it was all clear, I became that girl. You know the one, the girl that didn't care about anything. I had the confidence thanks to long talks with my older sister. I had the courage to try things because I had already been down the road, but most of all, I had the talk and the walk; and you best believe the walk was fierce and the talk was slick. I could walk in any club or bar, even being underage, without being carded, and the men seemed to fall at my feet. At first I was overwhelmed, but then I grew to indulge in it and use it!

One night I was introduced to two guys, but I was so wasted I couldn't decide which one I liked more, so I chose them both. For the next two weeks I was treated like what I thought was a queen, wined and dined, delivered flowers and gifts without even having to give up anything, if you know what I mean. I learned that in the midst of all that was going on, my heart was not something to be toyed with, because within this temple was a rare and precious gem that I would soon learn that men looked for and wanted to possess, but I needed to learn more. I needed to do research on this precious gem and find out its capabilities.

For the remainder of my vacation in Georgia, they were like little lab rats, and I was the scientist. I watched men talk, the way they moved, the way they dressed, their attitudes, and demeanors, not because I wanted to be one or even think like them. I wanted to be the ultimate woman I could be and, just like men, get in touch with their feminine side; I was about to get deeper in touch with mine as well as my masculine side. I read books about sex, I watched pornos, I started thinking back to the nights in the club and the conversations with the ladies, the different tricks and seductive tactics. I did this for about 2.5 months and was still learning when I returned home, but now I had put away my Converse and was now in that space where you can't decide what to wear or what shoe will work, so I decided to change the fashion game. Sneakers and tennis shoes no longer appealed to me. I was done running. It was time to strut.

As I lay there next to him as I had done so many nights, I smiled. I can remember dreaming about this night when I was fresh out of high school, not necessarily the sex but just wanting to be in his company. Back then I had a major crush on him. Hmmm, him we will call Louis because he was timeless, aged, and a classic like Louis Vuitton shoes, not to mention thirteen years older than me. I remember telling my mom that when I get out of high school, I'm going to have that man, and she would always respond, "And what about his wife?" Yes, his wife; and I would always respond that she's not my problem. He has to deal with her. But I was young and said it jokingly because deep inside, I never thought I would have a chance. I knew that for quite some time they had been having marital issues while I was in high school, and even when I returned from college, I would see them and knew. I would hear the stories from my mom and their friends and even from his mouth a time or two, while I was ear hustling, about his infidelities and unhappiness, but it wasn't until that one night that I saw a glimpse of light. As I sat at the BBQ that night, I was in deep thought about going out to the club and what I was going to wear when I heard a sort of whisper: *Brandy*, *Brandy*, then it became a yell. This time I heard it. It was my mom calling me over to the table with her and the couple throwing the party and

Louis. His wife was in another room. As I slowly walked over, I heard the hostess tell Louis, "Yeah, she's had a crush on you since she was in high school, and we told her she was too young. Ain't that right, Brandy?"

He smiled and said, "You are far from that little girl I remember."

And I was real cocky when I told him, "Yeah, far from it."

And I walked away and right into his wife who said, "But yeah, she's still just a lil girl though," and she gave me this look, like she was putting me in my place or that I was chartering shallow waters; and I looked back at her with the same look because now you are in shallow waters, because this is one girl that wanted to be pushed overboard and you shoved her at just the right time, and I had life jacket in tow because swimming was not my thing. I was more of a floater.

That night I headed out to the clubs with my girls, and as we exited the last club of the night, he approached me in the parking lot and said I shouldn't be out that late and he would give me a ride home because my friends were still roaming the parking lot. I walked over and told my friends I had a ride and would call them. And as protective as they were, they wrote down his license information, as they said, just in case. We drove in silence for a while then he slowly started to converse, asking me about leaving college, what was I doing with myself, and was I working. Questions I didn't feel like answering because I was wondering what is he up to. Although I had a small inkling of what it was, but I was gonna play this out.

Ladies, if there is one thing I have learned about vintage, it's that they are contemporaneous, aged, and have had a lengthy existence, so I needed to tread lightly because I was dealing with what they call old school, and you have to use care when handling. I was very short and quick with my responses and was relieved when I looked up to see we were at my mom's house. He stepped out and came over to open the door.

First thought, *Oh my, I am out of my league*.

He helped me get out the car. Second thought, his hands are really big and soft.

He leaned over as I was searching for my keys and grabbed my cheeks slightly and asked, "Are you sure you're ready for what you really want?" Third thought, I stuttered, said no, and ran to the front door.

Damn, what just happened?

He walked over to the door and whispered, "I won't take you anywhere you're not ready to go, but just know I heard you," and he reached over and kissed me on the forehead and said, "I will pick you up Saturday for dinner. Think about it for now, and you have a week to let me know."

I went in the house, told my mom, and on Tuesday I called to say I would go. I had now stepped into the zones of adultery and sin. I knew it was wrong, but I made excuses of why it was right. They're separated, she doesn't love him, and eventually these excuses went away because I didn't care. I lost that compassion when I lost my virginity along with my faith. I smiled because, yet, another had bit the dust, and yet I was still learning, but now more so. I was learning what it took to please a man from an older man. This man made my legs tremble, a feeling I only heard people speak of. I lay there because I felt numb. He did things to my body that made me want so much more. He made me feel like he was the definition of sex, and then there was a knock at the door. I put on one of his T-shirts and slowly walked out of the room. As I walked down the hall, I hear arguing. The voice sounded so familiar. They were going back and forth, back and forth. Suddenly I froze in one spot and wanted to turn and go back to the room when suddenly a light came on, and I was now standing face-to-face with the wife. After accusing me of sleeping with her husband all these years, being a home wrecker, and any other name she could come up with, I stood there, looked her in her face, and laughed. I then turned and walked back to the bedroom. For the next five minutes I listened to her tell him how he was robbing the cradle and how could he sleep with his friend's daughter and listened to him stutter and keep telling her to leave, till I had enough. I searched the room for my things, grabbed my overnight bag, and headed for the door. I waived and he asked me not to leave.

She said, "Let that b—h go."

He yelled, "There's no need to call her out of her name," and turned to me again and said, "Please don't go."

I opened the door and walked out, not because I wanted to leave but because I wanted to show her that she had no control over him anymore, but this time I gave her that look that she had given me in the past to let her know, "You are now in unchartered waters." There was something inside of me that was controlling his emotions and movements. As I got outside it was at that point I remembered that I didn't have a ride because I didn't have a car or a license…he had picked me up. Damn!

I was probably gone for about two minutes before I heard him call out to me, "Brandy, where are you going? I'm your ride. She came by, picked up the dog, and wanted to argue and be extra as usual, but she's gone, so please come back; and if you still want to go, then I will drop you off."

I walked back, heard the door lock, and suddenly turned around. There he stood, six foot four and I couldn't walk away. He grabbed my bag, took my hand, and said he was sorry as he gave me the coveted kiss on the forehead, which he seemed to do quite often. Now for those of you that don't know, the kiss on the forehead is that sentimental kiss of seduction. Here I am thinking I was in control, but I was at a loss. One minute I'm standing in the doorway, the next I'm straddled over him in a recliner about to reach the second climax of the moment, and oh my...

One thing we as women don't like when it comes to our shoes is we don't like replications or counterfeits, and Louis Vuitton truly fit this man. Although several men came after him, it was impossible for them to bring me to the heights of wisdom, sexuality, and spiritual depth that he had. Like the brand, he had learned how to retain value.

As years passed, I studied men, learned from men, and some of the best I would have to say. I became one of the boys, mentally and emotionally, and soon learned to separate the two from sex; and as time passed, I learned to separate me from it all. I became man's worst nightmare, but I was still learning myself, so there were some flaws and some details that I needed to still work out and work on.

We as women seem to be like flowers. We start off as a seed, you nurture and care for us, then we bloom into something beautiful that the world can't wait to see. I am a rose, beautiful to look at, but if you get too close, you are bound to get pricked by a thorn; by now I saw what they saw, men and women alike, I saw a beautiful rose that was beginning to bloom and grow. There was still a part of me that was on a personal mission, searching for something deep inside that hurt, using something deep inside that gave men pleasure and could make a grown man change things about themselves that they normally would never do. I loved from below the waist instead of above, and men smelled the essence. Brandy was that girl, not yet a woman but indulging in the things in life that robbed her of her innocence to love and feel love. Her demeanor was quiet and laid-back. She was naive and full of life and energy and wanted to learn what the world had to offer, but she started to see only the pain that she had been shielded from for so long. This newfound independence was not as exciting as she thought it was going to be.

I was that girl. I looked in the mirror and I saw beauty, a godly creation full of hope and promise, but when you've been burned and hurt so many times, your reflection starts to appear a bit hazy. The image you see may or may not be what you are really looking at but a disguise, and this was one disguise that was going to take me far until I learned to evolve...and evolve I did. Somewhere in my life, something had ignited a flame, and I continued to throw more fuel to let it grow. I was about to not only light it but let it burn and watch as well as be the one to ring the damn alarm. I had finally had enough or had I?

Simone

BEAUTY IS IN the eye of the beholder, and the only eyes that mattered were those of my own. I am drop-dead gorgeous with a smile that could make any grown man drop to his knees. My every move is calculated and precise, and I know that they're all watching—men and women both—whether it is in hatred or lust…hell, I didn't care. I've travelled a long road in life and know I deserve so much more, but I am damaged goods. Constantly returned back like a piece of unwanted article of clothing, worn and washed with nowhere to go, my life was going nowhere, and I needed a change—change from the normal guys in the area, change from using people to get what I wanted. Dated the guy at the shoe store so I could always get free shoes, but my favorites seemed to be those at a distance because they couldn't judge me, but the only problem was

I still felt empty inside. I would look in the mirror at times and see this beautiful specimen, but I hated her at times because she was lifeless and seemed to be going nowhere, and I wanted more! The scariest part of it all was the fact that she lacked fear of anything and this is what I loved and what gave me passion and drive.

As tensions in my life started to rise, I knew I had to get away. Things were becoming overwhelming, so instead of doing what I did best—running—I thought about things and put together a plan because now that my visions was clearing, I knew I had options. I decided that if I am going to do something, I am going to go all out and once again change the game. If there is one thing I had learned, ladies, it's that you can reinvent yourself at any time in life. We are equipped with the tools to be able to change our situations by putting yourself in better situations. This lifestyle had me lacing up boots, and not just any boots, but the kind that gave you a sense of discipline in your life and gave you a chance to fight for something and do something to make a difference.

Simone commanded attention from day one. She knew what she wanted but needed to figure out how to get it. She was a long way from home and marched away into the ranks, right into the military where her life was now just about to begin, and the learning experience was about to take on an all-new meaning and experiences that would push her beyond her limits and question her morals and ethics even more. Simone knew a smile, especially hers, usually went a long way especially when she wanted something bad enough, and she truly lived by the phrase, "Closed mouths don't get fed," so she did what it took to survive; and just like the environment she was in, she camouflaged her life and started a new life, in a new city, new state, and new game.

Ah, to be young and not have a care in the world, this is great, and I loved this life! I wake up early, work-out, go to work, and then come home and chill—no worries, no problems, and no concerns, but most of all, no drama…where has this moment been all my life? I had a roommate who was very open to showing me the ropes of this new life, and I gladly accepted it. Still underage, there were several things I couldn't do, but that didn't seem to matter in this new life or environment. My presence seemed to be on several individuals' minds (especially the men). It's like walking into a prison and all they see is fresh meat in a sense. I laid low—the role of a true soldier—you learn your environment and the players in the game, and then you learn to adjust and to adapt. I was on the bottom of the totem pole in this game especially with the new players, some of which were in higher hierarchies. I had to map out a plan because this was a game of survival. I remember as a child seeing the military lifestyle and how cutthroat and devious people could be, but I also remembered the camaraderie and family feel it gave, and I wanted to embrace both without getting to far caught up; but mostly I wanted to learn to get to the top of the totem pole, which meant I was about to break ranks and question the hierarchy of things; but I prepped and planned and took a few hits, but they were obstacles. Even in the military you have to ensure your closet is always ready for inspection and that your shoes are aligned and shined.

My only thought was how good I made this uniform look. Some, upon first glance, thought I was conceited, and around this time, I was but with a bit of cockiness. In my eyesight, I was that chic that all the men wanted to know and be around, and you couldn't tell me anything; but in my mind, I was lost and still searching for something.

I remember my first night going out with my new associates. It had been almost five months since I had taken on this new lifestyle, and my roommate thought it was time for me to stop hiding and get out and mingle. But little did she know, I wasn't in hiding. I was studying and waiting to see what this place had to offer. That first night was like feeding candy to a baby as I sat back in the corner and watched her work the room. My roommate, she was very much like me in so many ways, but where I was more reserved about what I was doing, everyone was so into her business that it was sometimes hard to cover. I did not mind playing the back role during this time because I knew I would have to jump soon. I will admit, though, at times the barracks felt like college-dorm life and will admit my roommate was a bad broad, mentally and physically, or as I used to say, "If I was still in that life, she could have got it!" I felt the eyes on me and heard the whispers and whistles as I walked slowly around the club, but I kept eyes front at all times, but my peripheral was a mother sucker. Inside I laughed as I heard the "Man, that's her" and "What's her name and her story." No one knew anything about me, and for the meantime I needed things to stay this way. I was that mysterious chic that men were beginning to fantasize about and was on everyone's mind and radar. I left that night and started to put my plan into action, and when my roommate thought I was weak is when I enlightened her.

Some ladies sit in the corner because that's where they feel they belong. Some women stand in the corner for safety because you have your back up against something, and you can see everything going on around you; and then very few women stand in the corner because they want to so that they can be pulled out by just the right person. See, ladies, there is nothing wrong with being weak sometimes. We have all been there, but you have to consider the obstacles or entities that are causing you to be weak, and once you clarify this, then you come up with a solution to build strength to be able to not only stand but to have stamina and endurance for the upkeep. My upkeep involved policies, regulations, and knowing the rules outside the rules to be able to stand with the hierarchy, because someone was about to be replaced in the ranks as I saw it. Now the thing about going up the chain, you have to know what the consequences are. For example, if you wear a pair of thigh-high boots in the summertime, your legs will sweat, but in the winter they stay warm—environmental adaption. If you run across rocks, you don't wear stiletto boots. You find Timberlands, and when you go to war, you wear combat boots, depending on the war and the individual. For me, love was a game that had to be played with calculated moves, sex was fun but had to be used cautiously, and romance was obsolete—at least on my end it was, but it was more about the seduction.

Something I had learned early on is that when you want something so bad, know the rules of the game, and when you profile your source, make sure they have something to lose other than you if things go sour, because if not, you end up back at the bottom. Most men of hierarchy protect themselves and cover well, so you have to be sure that you look carefully for that tactical boot—all terrain, protective insole, and with good height. I believe eight inches is standard.

He was not my normal, the preppy, educated, pretty boy type; but he, just like I, was just starting out, but we were in two different worlds. That first night we danced, laughed, and discussed our likes, dislikes, and differences and eventually the things we had in common. He was my penny loafer. Loafers are comfortable, but he shined and brought knowledge to my life, and behind closed doors, he began to show me things that I didn't know I was capable of. I indulged in this learning experience, indulged so much that I was blinded by things that were going on around me. My entire day was starting to be consumed with his schedule. I no longer had free time. It was his time. From movies to shopping, driving lessons to museums, or just weekend-long sexcapades, we were always together. Mister Loafer was there from the time I got off work till the time I fell asleep at night, but due to our positions, he never stayed over, but he made sure everyone knew I was taken. On occasions I would still hear guys talking about me, and from time to time one would actually have the balls to speak and show that they were interested, but the conversations always ended the same way with them being more concerned about the relationship I was in and not the relationship I could possibly be in. A part of me was starting to fall for loafer, but I wasn't sure if it was because of the possibilities of what could be or the lust; but as time went on, I started to show in the form of lust because I wanted more, and I knew he couldn't give it to me. We knew that the day was fast approaching for him to leave, and we had no idea where this relationship was going to head, and he was all for making it work and seeing where it would go, and I agreed. A week later he was gone. We went several weeks on the telephone and talking, and then the weeks started feeling longer and our conversations got shorter, and I knew something wasn't right. One day I decided to do some research and used my resources to see what was the real story, and this story I was not quite prepared for. Not only was he married but he had a child…end of story, end of fairytale. Reality just hit, and you just brought up a wall that was going to stand taller than the Berlin Wall. The next few conversations were very subtle until he said he wanted to come and visit, and I agreed. It was as if things hadn't changed, and I needed him to feel that way.

The conversation was planned. It would be short, quick, and to the point, "You lied. You're married, and I don't even want to know when you were gonna tell me or why you hadn't told me from the beginning. I want you out my room but, most of all, out of my life."

The response caught me off guard, "I'm sorry. I only thought this was going to be a one-night stand. I never thought I was going to fall in love with you, and I definitely wasn't sure if you were serious about this until now."

I laughed and walked to my door, and as he walked over, I kissed him on the cheek and said good-bye. Loafers no longer went with anything in my wardrobe, and besides, how could I be a soldier marching around in loafers? They did provide comfort but more so from the totem pole standpoint, but I needed a shoe that stood out; one that said POWER and "I am here!" Now it was time to go shopping, and I had several shoes in mind that I needed to try on and a few in particular that was in sight that I wanted to purchase. It was time this installation knew Simone was here and that I had no problem turning you down at parade rest or even having an officer or two stand at attention for me. I commanded respect when I entered the room, and I demanded attention and would settle for nothing less. Forward march!

Wow, my very own and first pair of combat boots. Now these boots were all-weather and versatile. They weren't the tactical ones I needed. They would serve a better purpose, but most of all, it appeared on my doorstep unexpectedly. Boots was quiet and very respectable but had a hidden agenda that would benefit him. We met through a mutual friend. She was dating his friend and thought we would hit it off well, and indeed we did. We were inseparable, literally inseparable. We enjoyed each other's company and looked for clock out time to see each other and just chill. I felt so safe, but most of all, I had found a pair of boots I was comfortable in and that I could trust to not leave my feet hurting at the end of the day. We would lie around for hours just talking about the future and our goals and expectations. Boots was a camouflage lifer and was very into his career and where he wanted to go with it. We discussed my ambitions, and he started showing me ways to better myself. We studied together, ran together, but most of all, we were together. Now this is where my mind began to take over my body because I was now absorbing all of this intel that boots was giving me, and I would one day put it all to good use. Just like most things in this career, it was short-lived due to movement once again, and although I tried the long distance thing, it did not work and it wasn't in the game plan because it took to much attention to try and keep it up. However, boots left an impact on my spirit and my mind but not on my heart because this is when I realized that long-distance relationships and I were not meant to be because I had a thirst to love and a need to be a part of someone's life, but I was slowly realizing that I had lost control of my own life and was heading down a road that led to heartbreak and disaster. Everything I touched or everyone I seemed to come around was making me feel as if I was the problem. Girls hated me because I was bold, confident, and obviously beautiful. Guys wanted me because of the same reasons, and I was at a crossroads where I refused to fall for either, so I rebuked them both and lived this out-of-control life until it brought me to the lowest point in life in which a person could get to. As I sit in this room, tears running, I'm wondering how I got to this place. I see people all around me, moving fast and talking even faster. A nice-looking gentleman stands in front of me, asking why anyone would do such a thing. There are wires everywhere, and the taste in my mouth is horrid. What the heck is going on? Outside the door I see a policeman and a familiar face. I try to focus to read lips but no luck, so now I try to think back and remember. I look up and try to move, but it is painful. Finally I get to the bathroom, I look up into the mirror, and now I start to remember. It becomes overwhelming, and I black out to awaken to several nurses and then I hear it, "Why would such a beautiful girl with so much potential want to take her life? What can be so bad?" From this point I vowed that I, Simone, will learn to love myself better and show more respect for my temple.

As days passed then months, I was finally starting to grow into my own, and I loved the life I had created, but I was starting to hate the body that I was in. My looks in the mirror started to have more frowns than smiles. My attitude was getting uglier, my personality was starting to reflect this, and suddenly I found myself in a depression. The bad part about being in a depression is when you don't know you're there. My problem was I was there and thought it was a part of my life or at least the way life was to go, but I was wrong. I have always heard that God puts people in your life for a reason, but over the past few years, my faith was starting to feel so nonexistent that I didn't know what to believe.

One night about a year prior, I remember being so sad. My roomie thought that it would be good for me to get out and go to the club to just chill, and I must admit we had a great time. As we walked out the club that night, my head was down as it normally was until I heard a deep but yet calming voice say, "When God blesses you with a face like that, it's for the world to see, so please hold up your head." My first thought was to say something smart, thinking he was shooting lines until I looked up and realized he had kept walking, which meant he was not interested in me that way but was genuinely making a statement. I looked up and smiled and said thank you. That night he was on my mind, and for several nights afterwards, he became my Timberland. Now Timberland was your stereotypical East Coast type of man from Baltimore. Now when the thought came to mind, it was because he was rugged but real and slightly rough around the edges. This was the type of man that would stomp through the mud for you, hike up the ups and downs, and have your back; but you know Timberlands were a quick fashion phase and came and went. Two weeks from the day we met, once again walking out the parking lot, we glanced, but this time our eyes met and he stopped. He asked if it would be okay for him to take me out sometime. We exchanged numbers, and everything in me was wishing he would call. The next day he called. We talked on the phone for hours about everything, and we set a lunch date for Wednesday. All week I waited anxiously to meet up with him. We both had an hour lunch, but I was disappointed because we both had to be in uniform. He picked me up from the office, and we headed to a close by fast-food restaurant. He kept time-checking and finally told me that as an NCO he needed to set the example and didn't want to make me late. I was a private. After that date we spoke frequently, but because of our conflicting schedules, it was hard to try to make a date or any type of arrangements. One night during football season, I sat in the lounge of our barracks with a few of the other soldiers, and all I remember is a bottle of tequila and everyone taking shots back-to-back. It was finally down to me and the two alcoholics of the unit, but finally it was too much…I excused myself and went straight to the bathroom and then my room. Suddenly I felt uncomfortable and wanted to be somewhere I felt safe. I called Timberland to see if he would come pick me up. After laughing at me for a minute he said, "I will be there in about ten minutes to get you." In exactly ten minutes he was there. I slid into his car, and he looked at me and just laughed and asked, "SiSi, what was you thinking? You're not a drinker." I slowly passed out during that quick ten-minute drive to his barracks. Suddenly the car stopped. I felt him pick me up and carry me for a while and then he laid me down on the couch. Some time during the middle of the night, I woke up but I was so out of it. I saw him sitting in a chair next to me watching TV, and I noticed my clothes had changed. He told me that he changed me because I reeked of alcohol and had given me a shower, which explained the wet hair. He helped me get up and walk to the bathroom and then pulled the covers back and laid me in his bed but not before he sat a trash can on the side of the bed. I think I threw everything that was inside of me up that night, and he laid there with a warm towel on my head and holding my hair back with each turn. About 9:30 p.m., he gave me a bottle of water and two aspirins, and I went back to sleep. Around midnight I was able to put something in my stomach without it coming back up, and finally I could have a decent conversation. We lie in the bed and talked for what seemed to be forever. At three o'clock in the morning, we had our first kiss. After almost 2.5 months from the day we met, it was about to go down. We had sex until the sun came up, fell asleep in each other's arms, and when I finally did wake up, he had breakfast laid out and a kiss on the forehead waiting for me, and I finally knew what it felt like to truly be wanted. About two weeks later I received the call from Timberland, telling me he was being sent on a mission to Thailand for three months, and my heart dropped like a bag of rocks in the ocean. During those three months, I went through so many emotional roller coasters, and oh, the shoes. I must have gone through so many due to size or defects, but it was always something they lacked. The newer shoes lacked that worn feel, the price didn't reflect the worth, and the styles weren't rugged. Somewhere between the Mary Jane's and the Air Force Ones, the shoe styles and trends went downward, and I was now looking for a new pair of boots.

I've always had a habit of having a backup shoe in all instances, but now I had a new style I was going for. I had a new outlook on life, a new found freedom, and a new roommate. I liked to call her Colombia like the exotic country, not the shoe brand. Colombia was beautiful, her accent was exotic, but her attitude was young and a bit naive, but she was a quick learner, and we got along great. A match that no females could mess with and a bond that would last forever! I remember the first time she talked me into going Salsa dancing. It was hilarious because she moved so smoothly with a sexy vibe as she twirled and flipped and dipped, and I was in awe, and I soon learned. From her is where I got the idea of wearing the knee-high length boots. Soon I also had a new friend. He had been around for a while but stayed in that friend zone as we call it. That quiet brother that hints to you but is so intimidated and afraid of rejection that they don't step to you 'cause they feel you may be out of their league. I was so busy looking through and past him that I never took the time to look at him until I found myself in the valley, and it was him that I turned to for comfort. That comfort came in the form of listening to me vent or just lying with me at night or holding me when I needed just a real friend of the opposite sex. It was crazy because I remember trying to hook him up with Colombia but found myself getting mad and jealous at the fact that he would come over and hang out with us or go out dancing with her when she just didn't want to go alone. He was that type of friend. Colombia wasn't interested in him, but he was a cool guy to be around. Like I said, he was that type of guy. One night Colombia stepped out on faith, as I call it, and asked why we weren't a couple, and I had no answer. See, as cool of a guy as he was, he was a troubled individual, always in trouble behind childish things, or what I considered immature. He was still running with the crowd, fighting and acting a fool in the streets with his boys, which is why we will call him a Nike, not because he was a phase or because of the different variations of his personality and the man that he was, but because of the man he transformed into later in life made him stand out as a Cole Haan. Those that love shoes know the story and the relationship between Nike and Cole Haan, so you can appreciate and understand where I am coming from when you meet this type of guy. He is a forever-friend. You meet at a bad point in life but for a reason, and then as you grow up and out and reconnect later, it's a magnificent experience, and time has stood still!

You see, my life during this time started to spiral out of control, and I loved every minute of it because I had a false sense of control. I had guys at my beckon call for anything I needed them for, whether it was to pay my bills, as friends, boyfriend's car note, or whatever; and I didn't care about their feelings. My conscience was clear as crystal, but at some point, even crystal cracks if you drop it enough or hit it hard enough, and I was about to feel that hit harder than I would ever expect; but it wasn't just one hit, it was one hit that brought back a compilation of memories, and that's when the crystal cracks and things aren't so clear. I got to a point where I wanted to try different things. Difference came in the form of an unexpected relationship. Hmmm, we'll call him Hilfiger. And this was the crossover point that had the city in a buzz and a lot of brothers mad, and I loved it! I was happy and in bliss. I thought I had found the one and was in love. We were together day and night. Our relationship was the topic of a lot of conversations, some good and some bad, but we didn't care because we were in our own little world, and no one else seemed to matter. I admit there were times I slipped and I did what I wanted to do. The chocolate delight would be calling me, and I answered. At one point I can recall Timberland coming to visit me, and I walked away with him as Hilfiger stood by and watched, and I felt no remorse. But who would have known that karma would come in the form of a young lady that closely resembled Hilfiger's ex-wife. After a huge argument, we decided to go our separate ways, but before we did, I remember walking to go talk to him and the sight I saw in the window. Now at this point I wasn't sure if it was my ego or my heart that was crushed, but whichever one it was, somebody was about to feel this pain. Little did I know I would take it out on myself. Now, ladies, your boots are supposed to be able to get you through the cold, the rugged surfaces and make you feel comfortable or sexy, but my boots had been so poorly broken in that I found myself having to invest in the reinforced steel toes and heels to be able to march my way through the politics and bullshit of these fantasy relationships that I had formed in my head. I was a sexual beast, and I emulated sexiness, confidence, cockiness, and I wanted most of all to feel loved. And the funny thing is, all along I was thinking I was controlling things and was in control, but I was learning that these men were feeding off my energy, and they knew. So as I studied them, I learned to mask the emotion. And I must say I learned from a few of the best. These professors were from the streets of B-More, Philly, and VA—East Coast's finest, and their stature or sense of conceit was attractive, appealing, but also applaudable. And now I was ready in more ways than one to get my first pair of tactical boots.

It was so dark that morning, had to be about 4:30 or 5 a.m., and we stood there and I heard a different voice yell,

"At ease," as all soldiers went to parade rest. I could not see the face but I heard the voice, and it was a soothing one, and I wanted to see the face. Later that day I ran into the body, to put with the voice and now a face, And what a face it was. You know that feeling when you're in the store and you find the perfect shoe and then your song comes on over the intercom and you drop a bit at the knees, shrug your shoulders, and yell, "That's my song right there." Well, this was that feeling! I had finally made a major niche in the totem pole. We started out very, very slow, and one night he admitted that he was married but his wife was stationed overseas at the time and whether I chose to pursue this was entirely up to me. Little did he know, I knew his situation and that he should have been asking himself that question. Now I know this is the second scandalous and adulterous affair, but I will settle that with the man above. Some may judge this imperfection and behavior unbecoming of a soldier, but no sin or lie is greater than the other, and mirrors don't lie. This man truly had a lot to lose. Days went by then weeks then months, and anything I wanted I was given, and several friends benefitted as well from my spoils. This went on for about a year or more, but I began to get bored and was looking for other shoes because wearing boots all the time was not very fashionable and could sometimes get heated. I remember the night of the big argument. I was seen in public with one of his troops and it got back to him, and he turned to me and treated me like the private I was, and I was pissed. But more than that, I was once again enlightened because I had just realized that, regardless of what I wear, I am still the same when I put on that uniform—a private. All I could do was stare in disbelief and go to the position of attention and accept the consequences: extra duty. That night we met up, and he apologized and explained why he had to do what he did; and it was at that moment I realized that he was not the tactical boot I wanted because this was a point of weakness, and you were now a liability that I couldn't afford to insure any longer. As the conversation ended, I now gave him that coveted kiss on the forehead and walked away. Simone, a soldier in every aspect of the word, she led a life so disciplined that it was almost controlling. She was that chick that every guy wanted to know. Beautiful inside and out and what most would call sweet, but she had a fearless sense about her and a thirst to find love; and now she had learned the lessons, found the tools, and was now a creation of what most men feared and others were in awe of. And she was now a vision of a thigh-high stiletto piercing the hearts of all men and laughing along the way, not shedding anymore tears.

Now, ladies, at this point you may be questioning the shoes in your closets and feel the need to clean house and throw out some outdated or out of season shoes; but most of all, you are probably finding yourselves relating to these two women either now or at some point in your life. We have all had setbacks in life because of love, but it is because we are following our needs and wants and not necessarily what is meant for us or right for us. We all want comfort and the ability to stand tall, and this is why we compare our shoes to men because we are trying to do just that—find that comfort and stability in that one man. Now there are some women who clearly don't play by the rules or in a ladylike fashion, but then you have those who play by the rules until they are pushed to a certain point. I have stood in the mirror naked several nights and admiring myself, flaws and all. I have thought about the marriages I have intervened in and the relationships I have walked away from and questioned the reasons. Most women believe when they are in a relationship with someone that is taken that they can make the situation better or wait for that man to come to them, but the truth of the matter is this, when you mess with a married man, there are options to what may happen next: You either stand idly by and wait for him to leave, in which case most men won't, but if they do, you are now in the position that the woman before you was in; and it takes you back to the saying, "The same way you get a man is how you will lose him." You date a guy who is not married but is in a somewhat or so-called committed relationship, and he stays with you because 1) you are offering him the fantasy in which he feels he is not getting at home, or 2) you entered his life at a point when he is on the rebound, or maybe he just wants to sleep around. Either role you decide, let it be known because you don't want to be the one on the unknowing end, thinking a relationship is starting but it's probably not. It's sort of like the pair of shoes you put on hold or layaway because they are not in your budget but then you never come back. You should be tracking by now, shopping and relationships, men and shoes, and so many more accessories. One woman's life is no comparison to that of another's, but there are brief moments where you can see yourself in their shoes or know the feeling. But because you weren't experiencing the same thing or in the same frame of mind, you won't be able to feel the same buyer's remorse that she is now developing inside. Now we are beginning to grow and evolve into womanhood and ready for different experiences, so we need a fitting show for the journey, now enter the pumps, Maryjanes and the occasional flats of life.

Dominique

WOMEN HAVE BEEN considered as very unstable creatures emotionally and mentally, and some of us are, but then some of us know exactly what we want and how to get it…and some just know what we want.

Dominique was that one that go-to pump, or the shoe that gave you so much comfort. She was the one that everyone thought had it all, but she was broken. Beat down from life's constant obstacles in love, she lost the urge to live, to love, and for laughter; but she had others depending on her, and the overwhelming pressures would soon bring her to a crossroad. Dominique was one of those that knew exactly what she wanted…so everyone thought. She wanted a family, someone to love and care for her and fill that companionship void. Dominique had so much to give and so much to offer but was tired of running up against brick walls to get to it.

Where are all the good men at, is what I keep asking myself. God, just send me a man with no baggage and no drama. Is that too much to ask? I've had three proposals in three years. The first was what women call a red bottom. They cost a lot of money, and you only wear them for status, and this is what I call him because it was more of a status move for me in the beginning; and I thought we could grow, but unfortunately his status wasn't single, and I had to find this out the hard way. The second one wined and dined me, showed me what love could feel like and how I deserved to be treated, but he failed to tell me after he proposed that he was treating another to the same privileges including the engaging part. The last one—now I really thought he was the one, but I'm not sure if I was in love or just in love with the fact of being loved and put on a pedestal—his family wasn't ready for the crossover. Each of these relationships ended with a phone call to me and another woman on the other line explaining to me all the reasons why this would not work out, and I walked away from each one hurt and determined to find someone just for me.

I always considered myself a woman of very many talents and a wearer of several hats. My life has always been lived through film. I wanted the romance, happily ever after love; and in the beginning, I thought that was what I had; but in front of the crowd, I was happy behind closed doors I had lost myself. I had lost myself to a camouflaged, all-terrain boot wearer. He gave me protection, stability, but most of all, he gave me love. Things seemed to happen so fast in our lives from sex to kids to marriage, and we were inseparable.

He had his career and I had him and the kids, but I wasn't sure if that would be enough. I was so new to this whole husband-and-wife lifestyle. I listened to other couples, read books, and did research; but I forgot to go to God with it and read the one manual on marriage that counted: the Bible, and that is where things went wrong. My visions of being a wife were quite different from his. Yes, I cooked, cleaned, and took care of the kids, but my body was worn and my mind was torn; and it had started to show. I remember one day looking in the mirror and not recognizing the woman on the other side; and I cried, went into a depression, and my entire life started to revolve around my kids. Friends were far and in between because I wanted to focus on my family.

I remember the day I came to reality and became the woman in the mirror. I watched this man every morning get up, and inside my body I craved him, and I wanted to be around him 24-7. This man stood six foot one about two hundred pounds; his skin was smooth, soft, and chocolate; his eyes so mesmerizing, and his lips seemed to constantly be calling my name. Words just could not describe, so just imagine and close your eyes and think of it this way: If my legs were a dam, then the waters were constantly overflowing because the walls of the dam were constantly being let down to let him in. The sex was amazing, and there was such comfort on both of our ends. During this phase of my life, I was uneasy about a lot of things. My self-esteem was low; after having kids, my views on my body image were inconsistent in my mind. I was a cute girl, but on the outside I felt horrible; and to make matters worse, I had found myself in a situation.

The first time he didn't return home should have been a sign, but I went with the excuse, "Baby, I was so drunk and didn't want to drive home." The next day all he did was sleep. I went through his pockets and there were numbers...I threw them out and forgot about it. This started to become consistent to the point where we were constantly arguing. He being upset because of the fact I hadn't adjusted to being a wife and a mother, and me feeling it was unfair that he lived his life and could use the excuse that I don't know how to do this and I'm learning but it should come natural to you. One night we decided to go out. I hadn't been out in months, but I was beginning to slim down and feel a bit more comfortable about my body. I was excited, but that excitement would soon end in rage. I remember her smiling in my face and saying how pretty I was and how nice it was to meet me. We shook hands, and

I walked away…he stayed. This is where that naïveté kicks in because I sincerely thought she was being genuine. As I walked across the room, I turned back just in time to catch a glimpse of a kiss—not a forehead kiss, a kiss on the cheek, or a quick kiss, but a kiss on the lips mouth open—and my heart dropped. This is that moment when you're standing still and all of a sudden it feels as if someone has released the wrecking ball, and you're the target, but this time it hit the target dead on. One moment I was standing there, the next the jealousy, rage, embarrassment, and anything else I could feel through the numbness came through; and I snatched her and threw her. I was not mad only because of what happened, but because as a woman, I always thought that the bonds of marriage should be respected. And for you to look me in my eyes and talk to me as if we're cool and then do this, then you deserve to be dealt with. After I came back to reality, I placed my wedding ring on the table and said, "Obviously you made the wrong choice, and I am done." I wanted to be his everything. I wanted to define the phrase "I'm every woman." A wise woman once told me what you don't do another woman will, and until this point I had given him all of me and all that he wanted…so I thought. We had talks about sexual adventures; he wanted to be with a redhead…I bought a red wig. He wanted to be with a stripper…I signed up for pole classes and purchased a pole. He was excited about my desire to please and then he said, "You've done them all, but now I want to see…the forbidden." He wanted to be with a Caucasian? I couldn't bleach my skin without feeling I was somehow disrespecting myself and my heritage…think, think, think. I purchased some nude-colored body paint and a blond wig. He wanted a threesome, I gave it to him. But then things went to the next level where I was no longer involved, and it was at this moment of feeling and seeing this man for who he was that I decided I wanted more. Guess he didn't listen or hear the wise woman?

One problem that we as women have is that some of us allow this behavior to happen. If you allow a person to treat you like you're worthless, then you begin to feel like you're worthless. But instead of me feeling worthless, I felt it was time he got a tall dose of reality and his own medicine. I was now no longer seeing myself as lost in his image or his thoughts of me. I wanted to be everything he feared and loathed, but most of all, I wanted him to hurt. And now see the horns are out, and you're going to regret the late nights, not coming home, phone numbers, women calling our home, and even a few had the balls to come to the front door. My pain will now be your shadow.

Puerto Rico, I guess, was a tap shoe because he came tapping at just the right time. A new city, new job, and I was starting to feel myself. I started doing things that were out of the norm for me, but some days it felt so right that

I thought it was me. I masked my pain from my friends. The fights between my husband and I had started to get physical, but I masked the bruises and covered the truth and I smiled and said everything was okay and that we were happy and in love; when the truth of the matter was I was in pain, my insides were turning, and the thought of being next to this man I vowed forever to was disgusting me. As I walked out of the store one day, Puerto Rico stood there and watched. At first it was exciting, but then it was kind of stalker-like you can say. The next day he came into the store. He approached me and said, "I did not come in here to buy anything but to propose something." He handed me a box. Inside was a beautiful purple ring.

My first words were, "You know I'm married."

His response, "You didn't say happily, so can I continue?"

Now I was intrigued. He went on to say that he has seen me around town and noticed that I am never smiling or happy unless I am with my kids, and that a woman with so much beauty on the outside should be able to reflect her beauty on the inside with a smile. He handed me the ring and said, "This is yours to keep, and if I can't make you happy or at least smile within the next hour, then I will walk away and never bother you again."

This seemed like a win-win situation for me. It was, however, the longest hour of my life. We talked a lot, and suddenly I started feeling things I hadn't felt before, or at least felt prior to me getting married. He tapped his way right into my life, and I was beginning to make excuses for my lateness coming home or reasons to be at work earlier. This was becoming addictive and too easy, but no matter how deep I got into this situation, it didn't seem to mask the pain anymore.

Now my husband had a new friend. It was a bottle, and he turned to it more and more. He was great with the kids, a great friend, but a horrible husband unless things were going his way. I hated sleeping with him, but I did because I felt obligated; but in my head I would see visions of him with other women, and afterward I would stand in the shower in tears. One day as I stood in the shower, I had to ask myself who was I really hurting in this situation. He was getting worse, and I was getting deeper involved in a lifestyle I wasn't prepared for, and the lying and sneaking was killing me. Something had to give because I was tired. That day I went to Puerto Rico's home and had to tell him the truth and let him know I couldn't do this anymore. He wasn't the least upset and couldn't understand why I couldn't just walk away. And honestly, I had no answer except for the fact that I still loved my husband and until I knew I had given it 100 percent, I owed it to myself and my kids to try and make it work. I walked away that day with a guilty conscience but relieved that I didn't have to lie anymore. When I walked into my home, I looked

around, and it was a mess. I scrubbed that house from top
to bottom, started preparing dinner, went to pick my kids
up from daycare, brought them home, bathed them, and
prepared them for bed, and then we sat on the couch and
waited for their father—my husband—to come home. He
walked through the front door, and the look on his face was
one I hadn't seen since we dated. He walked over, kissed
me on the forehead, picked up the kids, and played with
them, and I went into the kitchen to get his meal ready.
After putting the kids to bed, he ate and then we sat there
in silence. Sometimes there are no words needed. You just
know things were meant to be right at some point. I was
raised to know that a man should be the head of a household and that a woman should never try to take that spot
or demean her king, but I took it upon myself to put man
before God and teach him a lesson through my pain. Was
he wrong for his decisions and choices? Yes, he was, but I
forgave him in a way that was convenient for me, which
was to get back at him. The moment I felt the love was
gone, I should have walked away, but I allowed the behavior
to continue because I thought I could fix it or that things
would get better if I just stuck it out. Sometimes we turn
on the music and tune everything and everyone out in life
and then we put on our tap shoes and go to a place and
time before the hurt and before the issues because it's a
nice comfort from the situation we are in. As a woman, I

continued to grow and learn more about him, the ideas of marriage in relation to the Bible, the true meaning of being a mother, and more. The journey was not easy, and there were several obstacles and trips along the way, but I went down the path. And even through the rainy days and the storms, I realized when the sun came out, I had grown.

Tatiana

TATIANA, SHE WAS the man-eater, independent, educated with a strong sense of self. She was the real deal, and she could walk into a room and make time stop but yet struggled to find her place in this world. Tatiana was the epitome of every woman. She possessed all the necessities and skills to get where she wanted and what she wanted, but sometimes her tactics were something to be desired or what some desired. Her thoughts were timely and calculated and what some would say was a man's nightmare, because she thought like them and could relate to them but had all the tools of a woman, and she used them well.

I love to be in the spotlight, but what I love even more is to walk in a room and just know all eyes are on me. I never carry a compact in my purse because I know what I looked like when I left the house, and when a guy compliments me, to most it would be flattering, but to me it's just, "I know, but thank you." Most would call me cocky and conceited, but I call it confidence and convinced. Trust me, there is a difference. I am the ultimate, the Louboutin, the Versace, the Prada of women. I can make fifty dollars look like a million dollars flawlessly! This road to self-love and self-confidence has been a long one, and although most would say that's not ladylike behavior, I would have to disagree because I am a woman of a different breed and believe that, other than the genitals, men and women are so much alike. The only difference is women hide it, society hides it, and men try not to recognize it; but the fact is that inside very woman is a part of man that came along with that rib, and I am very in touch and at peace with my portion.

I knew I was wrong, and everything in me as a woman was telling me to walk away, but I didn't because this is what I wanted, and I needed him to want me and think of me, although in my head I knew I didn't want to be with him. Sometimes it was just the challenge or the need to be wanted, even if it's temporarily. My challenge was the one everyone wanted. He turned everyone down because of his image, but I knew there was a blemish; and I worked it, exposed it, and eventually got him. He was my thigh-high, that exotic shoe that had to be worn with just the right outfit to make it look classy and not trashy, and we will call him Privileged. Light brown eyes that complimented his caramel skin tone, an East Coast swag that was so subtle, yet he was a mystery to so many; but what wasn't a secret was his situation. Privy was married, but on top of that, in a common-law relationship with kids with both women. This was supposed to be a very low-key relationship, and for a while it was, but like the old saying goes, "What's done in the dark will soon come to light!"

One night I stopped in the club to hang with a few friends, and you know how it goes: you hear the music, the environment, and you start feeling the mood. He walks up to the table and speaks to everyone and then sits down, and we all start laughing and joking. As the night winds down and the music slows down, the conversation was all about how everybody wanted to dance with him but all was afraid to ask because of her. So in front of everybody I asked, and he took my hand, we walked out, and they all watched and whispered. The next day I was approached about the dance. Now normally I would do the woman-to-woman approach, but her approach was not a questioning one but more of a threat, and I don't do threats. Those are like challenges to me, and so I accepted. I clearly remember the day it happened. I was conversing with my only true friend, Baby Phat, about him and that I was going to get this man. I was also e-mailing him as well about a question he asked…well to make a long story short, the e-mails got mixed up, and I sent him one that should have went to her, and next thing I know we were at his apartment during lunch for a nooner. For those of you who don't know what a nooner is, it's when you and that select guy have sex as your lunch. What he thought was going to be a one-time thing had him in awe. In one hour he opened up about his relationships, the problems, and his goals as well as concerns. A part of me softened up from the hard part of me that was saying, "Damn girl, you did that. Now get your ass up and go back to work." These sessions seemed to continue, and he got deeper and more involved. He was showing up at my home at all hours of the night, and I would park his car in the garage to avoid questions. He would sleep over or come over early before work. Some nights he would call because he was drunk and needed a ride and knew I didn't want him tarnishing his "good guy" image. Things between us started to get crazy. I was taking him on sexual adventures he never dreamed of. There was the time we got caught in the park by security, and he was so concerned about me and my image, and then there was the surprise hotel room with the Jacuzzi and candles. Months went by and nobody seemed to know, but then he suddenly got messy. He slipped one night and said that four-letter word every woman wants to hear, except the fact I wasn't one of them because I was involved with another man or, I had conquered both challenges in this situation but was not ready for the confrontation. My career, my image, and my self-respect were on the line, and although I knew I was wrong, she needed to know she was just as wrong, and I refused to back down like the others. I felt like I did her a favor. I exposed to her that how can he be your biggest fan when he's cheering and supporting others and that it shouldn't be anything new. The new thing was the fact that she found out after the relationship was well over to bring this up and by then it was too late. I win, and I moved on to the next. I'm that type of woman that everybody talks about and condemns because it's not socially acceptable to have this type of attitude or behavior, but most of us have been there at one point or thought about it. I do it with no regrets, no remorse, but I do remember and that sometimes it's even worse.

Inside of every woman is another woman that is waiting to come out, but most of us choose to keep her secluded from fear of karma. The thing about karma though is that most say she is evil and scandalous and that she must be a woman. Well, karma is a man-made idea or thought I believe, and since I have always been high on my horse, I believed I was the bigger and the better woman, so I was not worried about her interfering in my life. Watch TV, the reality shows, lifetime, and the shows about women, they mostly show us as these emotional, crazy in love women, or they show us as these independent moms and go-getters; but look deeply into your life, and I am quite sure that inside of all of us there is a sexual beast, a Mary Jane, Olivia Pope, and professional sports groupie. We just don't show it or want others to see nothing more than a flawless image of beauty and brains.

I am the triple threat: brains, beauty, and body. I embrace them all, and I use them all to the extent that is comfortable to me and allows me to sleep at night, guilt-free and a conscience as light as a feather. Men fear me because I am like them, and also the women because they don't understand me. The biggest conquest was a married man, so I thought. I know this may sound bad, and with our girlfriends we would never discuss this because most of them would then start to look at their own lives and husbands a bit closer when that friend is around. My eyes were places higher in the ranks. If I was to go down that road, I needed one that had just as much to lose as I did—reason being, if things got messy, I knew he would keep his mouth shut to protect himself. This man was like a top shelf tequila in your drink that added just enough to make you think but not enough for you to lose it. We will compare him to our Manolo Blahnik, because it only took a little effort to build a long lasting connection and due to the quality of this man; but for short, he will be called Charlie. Now earlier I mentioned that I loved the man that every woman wanted but none dare cross the line. He was what they called visual eye candy. Charlie was this type of man. He was smooth (from his walk) to his car, the way he dressed, his talk, and was one of those where you didn't need to do a double take. He caught your attention at first glance and held it until he was well beyond your viewing site. The day we met, the entire office was in a buzz about this man; women running to the bathroom fixing their hair, putting on lipstick and lip gloss, top buttons of their blouses were unbuttoned; and I laughed, thinking what the hell is going on around here. As I laughed and stepped off the elevator, I looked up and we caught glimpse, I smiled, he spoke, and I continued on. No small talk. Baby Phat turned to me and said, "Well, you just saw why all these women were acting like a fool." And we both laughed and walked out of the building and went to lunch. As we were returning, we noticed a different car in the parking lot. One of the men was very familiar because we worked for him, the other was Charlie. They called us over, and as we strolled through the parking lot, I then started to notice what every other woman in the building noticed about this man. He was fine as hell! Something about me or my personality seemed to confuse men to the point where they felt the need to be honest. Now I don't know if it's because it was naturally in them, my charming personality, or from fear, but I loved this fact because it then put the cards in my hand, and I had an option. The option with this situation was that Charlie was very married and very well respected in his career, and then that's when the slot machine in my head went off. It wasn't the sound of money but the sound of stability and comfort and the not having any strings attached that was peaking my curiosity, but in there was some sort of connection. One late evening as I was sitting outside chilling with close friends, he drove by then reversed and called me over. I slowly walked over to the car, and he tells me that it's rare that he goes out but he would be out tonight and that he would love to see me. I had no plans on going out, but I told him I would consider it and thanks for the invite. During this time I was going through my own personal demons and didn't want to bring anyone else into it, but apparently he already knew and told me not to worry. At the last minute I got up and dressed and headed to the local club, a club that I can only remember coming to once or twice before then. As I slowly walked in, I saw my boss from the corner of my eye trying to get my attention. He ran over and paid my way in, asked if I wanted a drink, and guided me to a table as he placed an order with the waitress. A few minutes later as we sat talking, I felt a hand touch my shoulder and say, "Glad you changed your mind." We must have sat and talked for what seemed like hours, but it wasn't, as the night winded down and they played the last song. I asked him does he dance, he said yes but he was hesitant, but then he got up and took my hand. As we slow danced, the words to the song started to make me laugh, "Hey girl, how you doing, my name is Charlie, last name Wilson." This was our first dance, and that song was embedded, hence the name Charlie. This relationship spanned almost a decade. Unlike most women, I wasn't waiting for him to leave his situation, wasn't looking to be married. In a way I started looking at it me helping his marriage. I was giving him something he wasn't getting at home: an outlet or breakaway from whatever stress or frustrations brought him to my front door over and over. As the years went on we became closer and more of friends due to the distance. Occasionally I would get a phone call asking me to come visit if I could, or a "hey, I'll be in town. Can I stop through and see you." And I was fine with this arrangement not because I lacked self-esteem or needed love, but because it's what I wanted at the time, and it was on my time, rules, and convenience. Once I had a close friend ask, "How do you look at yourself in the mirror, knowing you are messing with a married man? Do the vows of marriage mean anything? Where is the respect?" I thought about what she said for just a minute, if even that, and I responded, "We all sin but in different ways. No one is bigger than the other. I look at myself in the mirror easily because what I see is myself. I have respect for myself, but why should I respect the boundaries of marriage if he doesn't hold it high enough a priority? Besides, when my time comes, it will not be man/woman that I answer to but God." As she walked away I could tell she was a bit upset and disappointed with my response, so I yelled out to her before she walked out the front door, "The only difference between you and I is that when you did it, you didn't know the man was married because he didn't give you the option. But I know. You got caught up emotionally, and you are the side chick that became the wife, and now you look down on every other woman that messes with a married man." Now, ladies, don't get me wrong. I truly understand the vows of marriage, but I also understand that what was put together by God no man/woman will be able to break or tear apart. So does that mean that their relationship lacked his presence?

We have all been that side chick at one point or another, either knowingly or unknowingly, depending on how much respect the guy had for you, but most of all you had for yourself. Sometimes we hold value to the wrong things, and we judge others based on our views or past experiences, but how fair is it? We will never be able to walk in another person's shoes or see life as they view it, but who are we to criticize or textbook critique someone for the lifestyle they choose to live. Mistakes are simply lessons learned, and you grow from them, and you will move on to make bigger mistakes or capitalize on the ones already made, but it makes you no less of a woman than the next.

There are several different types of women that we relate to: the strong, the successful, the courageous, the educated, and I could go on and on but I won't, because my path does not lead me to relate to a certain type of woman but to set myself aside and become what I like to call a whole other breed of woman—successful in life, love, and laughter; strength mentally, physically, and emotionally; educated in my weaknesses, faith, and abilities; courageous in my actions, growth, and well-being. My name is Tatiana, and yes, I am that one, the one you were warned about. I have studied men, watched men, and have accepted my rib graciously, but deep inside I am still a woman, and I have the same urges and desires as most. I just go about it differently. I know what I want and I go get it. I don't get it at whatever cost it takes. I get it because it comes easily, but sometimes too easy is not good, so I know when to walk away. I live with my guards up, but my walls are still soft. I walk with my head high and my stilettos even higher, and I have learned to run in them when it's time to run with the boys; and they sometimes fear me when I walk in the room, and oftentimes I just scope and kind of glance to look for what I call the next victim because that's what I view them as, because most times that's exactly what they're seeing me as. Soon though, I know I too will come across that one.

Awww man! I glance at the clock and notice I have been in this closet for hours, trying to clear out shoes and put things back in order to the point where I have exhausted myself. As I stand up, the aches and cramps remind me that I am no longer that agile twenty-something-year-old.

I take a quick glance in the mirror and see the reflections of Brandy, Simone, Dominique, and Tatiana in this thing called life in me. I have come a long way. Sometimes I stood separated, confused, but when I felt hurt or pain, I found something or someone inside of me to give me the strength of the one within that could get me through. There are many obstacles on this path to find faith and womanhood, but I, like most women, am still yet a work in progress; and at times we fall, but it is how quickly we have learned to recover then dust off and begin again that matters. Stripped of our makeup and standing tall, flaws and all, we are the reflection of the one in which we choose to see and choose to be. Women have travelled a path that at times there was no light because we had no vision. There was one thing though that we noticed: that our shoes always left marks to show we were there, and our marks were imprinted into the ground.

I am Brandy, young at heart, naive at times but bursting to find me. I am Simone, roughing it through life, taking the obstacles as they come. I am Dominique, played every role in life except the one of me. I am Tatiana, my tongue is sharp and my words cut deep, but I am in search of the words that truly matter.

As I reach to turn off the light, I look to see how far I have come, and I notice there is still so much more to clear out and sort; but tonight I am tired, and we will begin once again tomorrow as we go through the accessories and handbags of life called friends and associates. Besides, it's the weekend, and I need to get out and enjoy this life I have been blessed to be given 'cause Lord knows it hasn't been an easy one, but it sure has been an adventurous one, and I live it one way; simply stated…no regrets. I choose me!

www.ingramcontent.com/pod-product-compliance
Lightning Source LLC
Chambersburg PA
CBHW060256030426
42335CB00014B/1726